PRAISE FOR *AFTERWARDS*

In this stunning and unflinchingly reflective collection, Reagan Myers writes, "Just like that—the past has grown teeth and is hungry." *Afterwards* chronicles Myers' courageous grappling with the hungry past. Through necessary cyclical returns to the contours of coping with unthinkable loss, Myers teaches us what it means to grieve and shows us, with startling precision, the light of what it means to survive it.

—DR. STACEY WAITE, AUTHOR OF *BUTCH GEOGRAPHY*

Too often when we discuss depression and beauty, we use the word 'despite'. Reagan Myers knows better. With an honest flourish she declares that she is both depressed and still magnificent, broken and still worthy, human and still honest. In her first collection *Afterwards* she explores, with a plainspoken but undeniable openness, the truth behind what it means to be ourselves. She teaches us that we are not objects created by our brains and our experiences, instead we are imperfect forges capable of creating lives and legacies. This collection is not all darkness, Reagan laughs as well as she teaches, telling us what we need to survive anything our minds throw at us, reminding us to always have a 'battery powered lamp and a therapist'.

—JARED SINGER, AUTHOR OF *FORGIVE YOURSELF THESE TINY ACTS OF SELF-DESTRUCTION*

D0846589

In this full-throated and fiercely vulnerable debut collection, Reagan Myers navigates grief, sorrow, and depression with un-yielding wit and lyric precision. How does one move on after so much loss? And what does one do with the complicated desire loss leaves in its wake? Using compelling imagistic range, she un-shadows what lives between the hunger and life's demands, what it's like to be a young woman navigating body dysmorphia, remnants of an abusive ex, losing a loved one to suicide, and the early loss of a mother. While there may be "no map for moving on," *Afterwards* is the book you want by your side on the journey.

—JAMAICA BALDWIN, NEA FELLOW AND AUTHOR
OF *BONE LANGUAGE*

AFTERWARDS

AFTERWARDS

POEMS BY

Reagan Myers

Published by Button Poetry / Exploding Pinecone Press
Minneapolis, MN 55403 | http://www.buttonpoetry.com

For Margaret Jane Allen Greivel,
and for Drew Shifter.
This one has always been for you.

CONTENTS

Every occasion, know I'm ready for the funeral.

AFTERWARDS

HYPOTHESIS

There is no map for moving on.
Moving on implies *forward*,
and in this case, to move on
I must first go back.

The data set is not complete, so to speak—
there is no more relationship to be had,
only to be analyzed.

Does moving on require a hypothesis?
Safety goggles? Carefully placed labels?
It certainly requires a summary of findings;
something to be revisited down the road,
when none of this makes sense
all over again.

FOR THE FIRST WEEK

I either didn't shower all day or I didn't get out of the water
it's the illness that consumes you or you consume it
the fever that you break or that breaks you
there are some things you wash away and some things
you can only try to
his death lives in my skin and the soap cannot touch it

his death doesn't feel dirty but it can't be clean
the fresh wound and the scab
the antibiotic and the sickness itself
I think I try and wash clean what I can't make sense of
I think that sense has nothing to do with it
except the water—
so primal
the need for heat
the need for
comfort

ON SORROW

She shows up uninvited,
not quite a friend
knows where I keep the spare key,
reaches for the door frame and lets herself in.
She rifles through my cupboards, forgets to wash
the dishes, leaves nothing for me.

You know how a CD skips and skips and
sort of sounds sorry but really isn't? She can't help it,
she says. And don't I love her anyway,
how familiar her imprint in my sheets, how
after a while, I tune out her breathing like it is my own,
have stopped registering that she is not, in fact, me—

that it was not me who broke the glass
and left the shards for hours, not me
who used the unpaid bills as coasters.
She is the broken spot on my shower head,
she drips and drips, fills my ears. I hang up the towel,
catch a glimpse of myself in the fogged mirror
and see her, this not-sister,
this heavy ghost,
this me, not me, me.

MY THERAPIST ASKS IF SHE COULD WAVE A MAGIC WAND AND FIX ONE THING, WHAT WOULD IT BE

If I were alive in any other time period
I would be dead. My back is too bad to hunt
or gather, I can't hear out of my left ear
and lions probably approach from the left.
In the 17th century, my panic attacks would look
like possession: the shaking and the crying and the hysteria.
How many times does someone sob
"I want to be dead" before the exorcism
proves useless and you oblige?

DEPRESSION IS FUNNY LIKE THAT

This week, I sat in the parking lot of an Auto Zone and cried
for ten minutes straight because I could not change a headlight,
which sounds like a lead up to a terrible stand-up routine,
right,

and the joke is always on me,
like, haha, I ate half a bag of pretzel M&M's in bed
at 11:30 in the morning!
or I've watched the pilot of Gossip Girl ten times in two weeks
because I keep falling asleep halfway through,
because being sad is a goddamn joke sometimes.
This week,
my headlight wouldn't come on
and my first thought was "seems right,"
and I couldn't change it by myself,
because I'd have to take the whole bumper off or something,
and my first thought was "of course,"
or, "I wish I was dead"
because being this kind of sad is funny like that:
no inconvenience is a minor inconvenience,
it is all the end of the world or might as well be.

Depression is a silent film, a monologue shot underwater.
Depression is sulking because I refuse to talk to it anymore
by which I mean about it.

There are some days when I am so sad that
I don't remember what it's like to not be.
Like when you have a bad cold and you forget
how to breathe through your nose,
and are so sure you will never breathe through your nose again—
I am so sure I will never feel joy again.

Except, when you have a bad cold,
your job lets you call in sick,
and people tell you to get well soon
and there's a whole soup genre dedicated to your well-being.

I cannot call in sad to work.
Can't go to the grocery store and go to the sad aisle,
(which would only have like, already-stale popcorn
and the tea your best friend swears is good for you).
So, sometimes, all I can do is laugh.
If I don't
there might be nothing left.

There is a crack in my bathtub in the shape of the Platte River;
I know this because I sit on the floor of my shower so often
it has become a permanent imprint on my thigh.
I am there because I have a cold,
or because I have been sad since graduation—
not the last one, the one before.
Or maybe it's both,
but the cold makes the most sense for sympathy purposes.
I think I might stay here forever.
If I get out, I have to be a person again:
put on clothes, put lotion on my legs,
eat a bowl of cereal at least,
take care of this terrible body that refuses to take care of me back.

I am tired of talking about my depression as somebody else;
a ghost that haunts me and I am afraid of the seance,
afraid to know what it really wants from me.
My depression does not ask for much,
but when it does it is something I cannot give,
and that's the joke—
my depression is just me asking for something I cannot give.

I ask to come back to my body and it's only me saying no.
When people ask me how I am,
they might as well be asking where I've gone.

I am driving down a dirt road with no headlights,
When it curves, I will not know,
just drive on into the field.

My own voice on the radio
telling me there is no place for me here.

THE MONTH HE LEAVES, ALL THE SONGS ON THE RADIO ARE LOVE SONGS

this morning I threw up blood in the shower / but I cleaned my apartment for the first time in two weeks / & isn't that how wars are won anyway / with a little bloodshed / & besides / it's not like it feels unfamiliar / you know / the feeling of something leaving you / that shouldn't

PALEONTOLOGY

Isn't science about discovery?
The creation of new ideas, the unearthing
of old ones; and so writing this is not so different
than digging up a skull, finding his teeth.
How sharp they still are, even in memory,
even in words ow blank his eyes
o reminiscent of sitting
in the passenger seat,
even with his hand on my thigh,
even when we were not moving
he always looked straight ahead,
on to the traffic light or the next girl;
and that question or maybe
just this memory
will also someday become a specimen
to be unearthed, dusted off, catalogued—

There is nothing haunting about clean bones
and skeletons behind a velvet rope.

HOME

the laminate counter / the mixing bowl / the pots / the pans / the flour to keep from sticking / the cupboards / the sound of my father in the next room / the sink / my sister / the cinnamon / or the clove / the becoming that is bread / the oven fan / the kneading / the rolling / the purpose of my mother / the intent of care / i have always been here / i am always this age / there is something about my mother's kitchen / that makes me feel both fetal & unstoppable / the dough that is rising but not finished / what is childhood / if not ingredients to make something later / what is this kitchen / if not my yeast / if not what raised me

JUST LIKE THE MOVIES

In the movies the phone rings.
Someone else answers,
        they collapse to the ground,

they dramatically wail that he is *dead*,

and you find out that way.

There is a fainting couch,
smelling salts,
a dramatic reaction,

and a clear next step in the plot.
I find out by scrolling through Facebook.

When my best friend dies

I buy a bottle of cake-flavored vodka.
I drink it straight on my regular couch.
I call my mother and cry
and then I do not cry at all.

I am either crying or I have never cried,
the broken faucet or the unpaid water bill.

In the movies
there is a graveside funeral.

Everyone is in black and perhaps
it is raining or at least promising to.

In the movies I get to deliver a eulogy,
I get to say what he meant to me, but more importantly
I get to say goodbye.

In real life,
he gets no funeral because he killed himself,

his mother pretending up until this very moment
that something so embarrassing couldn't have happened to *her*.

I dream every night about a grave I have never seen,
a body I don't believe is real.

It has been eight months and his death still feels like a theory,
like a plot point in a movie,

like resurrection is possible and my useless brain can't understand
why it hasn't happened yet

because in the movies, resurrection is possible.

The character comes back in dreams, is always within reach,
is always a misplaced letter or an unread message or
a dream visit away.

In the movies, there is always a way to answer
that which is actually unanswerable.

There is no monologue to explain my grief.
I will not have a shining moment where I break through.

There is no peace in the finality of it all.

My grief is not a montage.
My grief does not feel like a cinematic device,

is not character development,
is not making me stronger or better.

Is just making me different.

Is making me heavy,
making me not screen-ready,

I found out my best friend was dead on Facebook
and not because he told me he was leaving.

And in the movies,
don't they at least say goodbye?

EVERY SIX YEARS EVERYONE IN NEBRASKA GETS A NEW LICENSE PLATE NUMBER

so next month, I am going to drive
by my ex-boyfriend's house and write his new one down,
assign sirens to a new set of letters and numbers.

How random abuse is
or, perhaps, not random at all,
        how conniving.

Last week the sheriff found a skull washed up from the Platte River
        because it is the rainy season again
the water dredging up past tragedies and reopening the case
        or the old wounds.

Just like that—the past has grown teeth and is hungry.

Just like that, the past is parked outside my favorite bar.

And knowing that is surviving,
is crawling away in the dark.

But at least
I am crawling,
at least
        I am alive.

THE GIRL BECOMES GASOLINE

A series of things that have happened to me on airplanes:

As a child with motion sickness
I threw up on the first eight flights I was ever on.
On the way to Amarillo, I threw up in my seat.
On the way to California, I threw up on my sister.
On the way to New York, I threw up in front of the bathroom door.

Last year,
I sat next to a man in a three-piece suit,
who loudly berated the flight attendants because e-cigarettes
"Shouldn't count as smoking."
Why are you wearing a suit on an airplane?
You sound like an asshole, and you look uncomfortable!
I am next to you in literally my pajamas.
You wouldn't need to smoke if your clothes felt like petting a
    hundred kittens.

On my last three flights
I've been seated in front of the plane's required screaming child.
Maybe it's a tired baby.
Maybe I'm actually the one screaming.
Maybe it's my vomit-covered sister time-traveling to haunt me.

On my last flight,
I fell asleep next to a man who looked like my father,
which meant I was not worried,
woke up to his wedding ring digging into my waist,
his hand on my thigh like an unwanted houseguest.

It is moments like these
I feel more sputter than storm,
more candle than bonfire.

Behind me, my friend Greg is asleep undisturbed.
In front of me, Ben is talking to a woman about her grandchildren,
and I, in the center of this plane,
am taking up too much space by existing,
am apologizing to the man next to me in hopes that this will be it,
that he will not follow me off the plane to my next gate
like the man did on the way to Denver,
or on the way to Minneapolis,
or on my way home,

or, the way across the country,
a man is reclining his seat into my fourteen-year-old sister's lap,
yells at her for her legs,
for having a body.
Or the way the boy in my geology lecture
follows me from seat to seat,
ignores empty rows,
puts his arm on mine,
mistakes my shrinking for permission.

Which is to say that my body is too woman to really mean anything.
Is too woman to be considered a threat,
is too woman to have a right to my own space,
or to have rights.

I don't know when I became a space to be filled.
My thigh an open lease,
my neck a wishing well,
and his hot breath, a coin,
a demand, cast into me.

So know this: each unwanted touch
is gasoline. Each prodding hand, flint.
Each time a man assumes my space
he is just stoking the flame.
And a spark, stoked enough,
will burn down the whole house.

ALCHEMY

In this dream, it's not Facebook,
it's a conjuring. Instead of
typing a message to a dead man,
I'm just chanting into a void.

One of those things has a purpose.
Facebook memories are the base metal,
the real memories, the noble.

Alchemists didn't only want immortality,
they wanted to be able to cure all disease.
Do you think the panacea includes
depression?

What about his suicide? Do you think
that my grief counts as affliction
with only one cure?

DENVER

we spent countless nights on the phone
& exactly one in the same bed

sharing a twin mattress in a silent dorm room
a too-small polyester comforter

neither of us slept for even a moment
sick with heartache and worried about what might come next for us

too scared to disturb the other
the light rail's horn keeping the time

I spent the years following that night laughing
about how ridiculous we were & how we were so nervous &

thinking of all the things I would change &
I will spend all of the remaining years of my life wanting to go back

to listen to you breathe
a thing I assumed to be fact

MAC MILLER

"I need someone to save me | before I drive myself crazy | and if life is a dream | then so are we."

In this dream,
I'm at the funeral again.
I say again, but I never went
to the funeral.
Not that one.

Some days, it feels as if
I always have a funeral to attend,
and some days, I feel as if
I've never attended one at all.
Depends on which grief
I am experiencing today.
I say today, but I mean
right this second.

Depends on whose casket I'm burying.
Depends on if it's a memory.
I say a memory,
but I mean I can't get closure,
so in this dream,
I am graveside,
by which I mean inventing a grave.

MAYOR DUKE

In a township in Minnesota,
a Great Pyrenees dog just got elected
for his third term as mayor.

I imagine leadership in its best form
looks something like that:
honest, unadorned,
willing to help because that's what it wants to do
and not because it has to.

I'm graduating this year,
and all anyone asks me anymore is what I want to do
with my life and I think I want to be kind;
to love with reckless abandon.
I think, given the chance,
I'd live my life a little more like Duke,
accepting what comes my way with joy.

ON JOY

We don't talk on the phone much anymore,
and I wonder if Joy has found something in me to be afraid of
(the way Sorrow has not.)
It is not her job to find me on the couch,
stroke my hair and remind me of what's to come—

Joy is a party girl.
Find her in bright lights,
find her all dressed up,
            glitter and shine and pink lipstick,
find her with something like champagne in hand.
Joy does not drink vodka,
Joy does not drink anything on the rocks,
likes fruit juice,
likes it when things are sparkling.

Joy does not do dull,
and that's me, almost always.
Joy is the cool girl
you want to be in high school
but perhaps are too afraid
to reach out
            and touch.

THE WEIGHT

My ex-boyfriend tells me I have gained too much weight
to *really* be attractive.
Says, no one will take me seriously anymore,
and I want a career, don't I?

The feminist in me is held hostage by my body dysmorphia,
she hisses in my ear that it is still possible to love every body,
just not your own.

The women in my family respond to trauma by not eating.
My dad leaves, my mom only consumes smoothies for three months.
My sister's boyfriend calls her one name too far,
all of her pants start sliding off her hips.
When my ex and I met, my high school best friend had jumped off
the tallest building she could find and I
was only eating blue Jell-O.

So when he tells me I have gained too much weight,
he is telling me I have gotten too happy for him to manage.
Prefers me broken. He is not the first man
to define me only by what he can handle,
only by what he can wrap his hands around.

MY NEIGHBOR VOTES FOR DONALD TRUMP AND I CANNOT HELP BUT THINK OF HIS WEDDING VOWS

Dearly beloved

    people

                entered   unadvisedly

but reverently

I take

          love   and   you

I take you

offer   to you   my faults

and   I   need help

            I need help.

I choose   my life.

To   hold   for better   for richer

'til death do us part.

MY FATHER SAYS

he'd never vote for a man / he couldn't trust alone / in a room with his daughters / and if that's what it takes / at least this final straw gives me value / and in this moment / progress looks like the empathy / of my father / who at the very least / will always love me / more than a party / so / in this moment / I know / we are / he and I / going to be / okay

NOW YOU DON'T

Father's disappearing act
needs no puff of smoke,

no sleight of hand, just a mid-morning
living room conversation.

There is no big reveal, no implied promise:
a door opens, a miraculous return—

Just my mother
sawed in half,

my brother asking all the wrong
questions, looking for trap doors;

my sister, captive audience,
waiting for ordinary,

for the end of the show.

I CANNOT LIVE SOMEWHERE THERE IS NO WINTER BECAUSE THEN I WOULD HAVE NO EXCUSE FOR MY DEPRESSION

My body is winter / my body is shatter / my body is the way you don't notice / the snow melt until it's gone / is the fallen icicle / is the wayward avalanche / my body is not my friend / is no one's friend / most days / my body is not even my body / belongs to nature or god or /

belongs to science / belongs to the cells that make it up / is a cold park bench / is an iced-over windshield / my body could use defrosting / my body is the car that will not start / no snow tires / maybe / my body falls like snow / muffled /

there is no chart for my body / no scale / my body cannot be measured / I have no concrete understanding of it / no one really knows the weather / I just ask her in for tea / ask her about her day because / there is no day without her /

My body does not know why it paints / an artist with no muse / settles for landscapes / calls them / self / portraits

STILL

Doesn't it sound like a joke—
The ex-boyfriend walks into a bar,
finds me on the stage looking a lot like a punchline,
or a target—
here to prove he is not out of practice.

When my therapist says "abuse,"
she says it like a question,
like something *I* should know the answer to.

Most days,
I am like a kicked-but-loyal dog,
I find myself following at his heel, even years later.

Even now, I hate myself for saying it.
For calling him abuser,
an honest name,
but one that feels like lying.
When a record skips enough,
that's the version you learn of the song.

And so my therapist says to forgive,
and forgiveness means I
will never stop going through the honeymoon phase,
that missing him erases all of his faults,
and missing him means that I love him, still,
that I love him chronic,
that the word *love* is easier to say than *abuse*
is easier than to say I stayed.
For years,
I made myself nothing but a part of him,
and I am always writing to both of us because of this.

Perhaps I still love him because I haven't separated him from myself.
Even now
I am both the bird's nest and the tornado,
the ship and the reef,
the human sacrifice and the priest.
And if I am honest,
leaving him was like watching my heart escape my chest
and finding it in my own hands,
and perhaps he is like a god to me.
Like a myth, elusive, but there is no fairytale
when he who makes you feel like possibility
also makes you feel like ending,
when he is both the prince and the dragon,
the true love who is always a frog.

He follows me out of the bar.
He follows me, for once,
and I keep walking
but I still text him afterwards,
tell him those poems were not about him.
And maybe they weren't,
maybe, for once,
I have been able to write about something that is not him.
Maybe forgiveness is not about him:
it's about loving myself without having to love him too.

But if I am being honest—
and I am being honest—
if he showed up on my doorstep tomorrow
I would let him in.
Smoke invading the house,
water seeping back into the carpet;
sometimes, this is the only visible sign of abuse,
the only thing left—
loving him; still.

"WHEN I LOSE THE WEIGHT"

there is a new stretch mark on the top of my thigh and
it is jagged and I cannot help but think of the tv shows
where the cartoon looks in the mirror and the joke is that
the character is so ugly the mirror cracks and it looks
just like this, looks just like this thin purple line,
and I can almost feel my mother
start a new diet from three states away.
isn't body dysmorphia a fancy way of saying i do not like
myself today, or yesterday, and cannot foresee liking myself in
    the future
even though I am trying.
I think losing weight too fast on purpose is the only form of self-harm
that people congratulate you for, so maybe stretch marks are
    the form
of recovery that leaves a mark; the ice cream hallelujah,
the proof that I am becoming again.

MAC MILLER DIES TWO DAYS BEFORE YOU DO

it made me crazy.
Might just turn

The devil
in.

I let   go but I never go with,
        okay?

        I'm here
            for you.
I don't do enough
Without you.

Had the homies with me, all the sudden they split

You know how it goes,
    one of these days we'll
    be afraid.
Think I lost

    the devil,
But   I always

            feel   like him.

    listen   to us.
                let me
Say my   bit:
            it made me crazy.

if you could see me now,
Love me.
my mind, it goes
           goes
       mad.
Might just

          let him in,

   yeah,
  let it go, but

  one of these days we'll all get by.
Don't be
      afraid.

I WEAR SPANX TO MY GRANDMOTHER'S FUNERAL

& sit at the farthest end of the pew because
I *love* my family and all but
this particular performance of grief is too
unrehearsed,
none of us hitting our marks.

but I do not stumble over the new testament reading because
even in death, I want to do my grandmother proud,
read these verses she may or may not have believed in
because this crowd of people need to hear it.
my grandfather, knees bent to a god he still believes
benevolent.

& perhaps I'm at the end of the pew because I have
not rehearsed how to hide my feelings,
or my grandmother died too suddenly for my proper grief-mask
to be finished,
so instead I wear shapewear to a Catholic church,
the same one my parents got married in,
the same one I got dedicated in:

my aunt, sitting next to me, whispers to me which
of the stained-glass windows are her favorite
and I like that window too because it's the only one I
can look at and not see an urn or someone crying.

The window has a single dove on it, flying
into the light or maybe away from it but it is
flying, and so, now, must I.

ON HOPE

Sometimes getting out of bed in the morning
is the closest I get to feeling hopeful,
the closest I get to the sun coming up,
a version of tomorrow.
Hope doesn't always make sense,
is irrational the way love is,
the way it is irrational that I am still waking up at all,
and hope is like that,
by which I mean is human,
is the way the body keeps running
despite the heartache, the deficiency, the misfire,
the way the heart keeps pumping
despite me telling it
not to.

IN MY FAVORITE MEMORY OF HER

we are sitting on the rocks in a park in the middle of the city,
the kind of middle where the cars are rushing
by and the dogs are barking

but that too is stillness.

and she is talking to me about art class, and the music she is writing,
and being happy again,

I am eating a salad and really actually eating
for the first time in weeks, probably,

she says we will not leave the rocks until it is gone.

she is pulling apart pine needles and is telling me
about the definition of worth, and in her definition,

I fit it.

her hair is in a ponytail and it is so strange for something about her
to be tied up and contained.

she is not wearing shoes, and I think now about
how her feet must have been burning,

but she stands there anyway,
stays there anyway,

and I eat the whole salad,
even though it takes an hour and we should have been in school
but everything around us is in full bloom.

she is smiling with all of her teeth,
a picture frame for her laughter

and in this memory she throws her head back when she is thinking
like the cat arching its back to receive the sun,

and in this memory I do not kill myself and neither does she.

I spend a lot of time thinking about what went wrong,
when she said "I haven't stopped crying since I woke up"

or "I cannot even imagine tomorrow"
and I was suddenly a child,

small hands,

unable to help her the way she helped me.

I think about the empty seat at her graduation,
the acceptance letters collecting dust,

and I have neglected these memories,
all the days where something went unbelievably right,

left them in the bottom of the dresser drawer
under the clothes I bought without her.

I think I am afraid that the good memories will hurt, too.
that I will think of the day she was so excited to hug me
she spilled coffee all over us both

and I will feel something other than joy.

just because someone you love has died
does not mean that they're gone,
it means instead of visiting the tombstone you go to the park.

the cars are still moving and the dogs are still barking
and she is playing her music,

but in my headphones now,

and I think that's the definition of the way she is still saving my life,
that she was so important to me
that even in memory she is my sweetest friend.

maybe the definition of us is how worth remembering she is,
not the funeral or the eulogy or the vigil,
but the coffee, the bear hugs, the sunshine that one day in May,

when she smiled with all her teeth,
and I did too,

and I do too, when I am telling this story of her,
the day we both took our shoes off,

and I took her hand,

jumped into the fountain,
leaving the world for just a moment,

and this time, we come back,
        together.

WHEN DEATH COMES

there is no grand moment, there are no questions answered or closure. when Death comes, it is because he has become impatient, because he is petulant. Death is a child and aren't we all just green army men in the sandbox—and just when you think you and Death have reached a truce, Death goes back on his word. Tells you better luck next time and emphasizes the *next time*. Death is a man who does what he wants and does not care for my opinion, just takes and takes and does not give me anything back except a wink and he probably says sweetheart, the way the slimy bartender does.

Death wears masks that look like my friends except it is never Halloween and it is never a joke, or maybe it is always a joke and only Death gets the punchline. Death waves at me from passing cars,waves at me from the tops of buildings. Death looks back at me in the mirror, flosses my teeth and reminds me that they are his for the taking because teeth die too, because everything dies. Death is the kind of man who chokes me in bed without asking first, lets me go and says I must have enjoyed it because I lived, didn't I?

Death is my ex-boyfriend who won't stop texting me. Death is all of the friends I wish would text me. Death holds all the cards and is a selfish dealer. Death is Vegas odds. I imagine that Death always looks nice. That he always has his shoes polished and a tie bar. That he is always dressed for a funeral.

I INHERIT PLANTS FROM MY GRANDMOTHER

that are both older than I am.

Both succulents, known for their hardiness,
for their waste-not-want-not.
An aloe vera plant is supposed to live
for a maximum of twenty-five years,
but this one is fifty at least,
a manifestation of my grandmother who, really,
should not have lived as long as she did.
There was the lupus, or the fibromyalgia, or
the Sjogren's disease, or the Reynaud's,
or maybe just being a woman in the 50's,
but there she was and here
is this aloe plant, which now lives in my spare bedroom,
and apparently has so many healing properties
that maybe it has transcended just a plant already, without
needing me to personify it-

The jade, though, is fifty and can live for fifty more,
and today, I noticed it had begun to sprout a new tendril,
leaves the size of my pinky toenail, which I also inherited from
my grandmother, continuing to grow as if
it did not know its caretaker was no longer with us,
or, perhaps,
because it knew that's what she would
have wanted.

TASK ORIENTED

month nine of grief therapy and I know I am technically not
where I started but this futon is starting to feel more and more

like square one.
or square two if that's what

even being in this office is.
I ask my therapist for more tasks to complete in order to

overcome the stupid sadness,
and she doesn't laugh and I think that's because she

is kind, but she does tell me (again)
that the only way grief works is that

it doesn't and it doesn't and it doesn't, and then
there is the light at the end of this goddamn tunnel.

POSTHUMOUS

Mac Miller releases a posthumous album and
I am angry.
"Anger is a secondary emotion" says my mother or maybe my
therapist but it is easier to hide behind the bluster of anger
than to break down,
or to admit that I am jealous of people
who loved a man that I have never actually met,
jealous that they not only have an album but that they
had a project, had something to do that they knew for
certain he would have wanted.

What do I do with all of these loose ends?
How do I quantify all of the aspirations
you dreamt of but never actually got to?
Put cover art on it, listen to it over and over
until I have excavated all of the answers:

How *lucky* to have that, to have closure,
Lucky, as if someone is not dead, but, then
he is and you are, and
I don't want to consider what I would give to
hear your voice again.

CHEMISTRY

Scientists say that you can tell how
compatible you are with someone
based on the way they smell.
I keep an almost empty bottle
of your cologne in my closet.
I clutch your old
long since washed t-shirts
to my face
hope beyond hope
I can still find us there.

ARIANA GRANDE CRIES WHILE PERFORMING IN FRONT OF THOUSANDS IN MAC MILLER'S HOMETOWN

Ariana keeps doing the choreography while she quietly sobs,
the lights glinting off her jewelry,
the mic picking up every small sound of tears,
and this is the closest metaphor for my grief I have ever seen.

When you love someone so totally they are part of your whole life,
then everything in your whole life is a trigger.

A trailer for a movie he would have liked.
A joke only he would have gotten.

Or, I'm having a breakdown because he is dead,
and I can't even talk to him about it.

But here I am, the music is playing,
people are counting on me,

the show
must go on.

THERE IS A MOMENT BEFORE THE STORM STRIKES

For Stu

where the air holds its breath, where the sky
is a quiet growl, bared teeth, and
at least for me,
that's when I know it is going to be bad—

The last silent moment before the world
or at least the clouds or
maybe just my own brain come crashing
down to the only solid ground I thought
I could call mine.

And then the storm is feral, is snarl,
pounding feet, relentless pursuit.
When I am in the middle of a storm, I can only think
of surviving the next few minutes,
the next lightning strike,
can only worry what will bring the blackout,
the loss of power,
by which I mean power over myself.

When the storm strikes, by which I mean
when the depression gets bad again,
I am at the mercy of the cell
but that doesn't mean I am unprepared,
not anymore.
I have a backup generator and water bottles in my basement,
a battery powered lamp and a therapist—

It took me all of this time, all of this
destruction, to learn

that weathering a storm doesn't have to mean that
you just sit and pray
for it to be over.
It means that you learn the patterns.

You watch the radar,
mark the calendar for storm season,
waterproof the foundation or at least
remember to take your antidepressants:

There has never been a storm that lasted forever.
There has never been so much destruction that
you cannot be rebuilt—
hammers and new electrical wiring and
soon, it will be the first day you haven't cried and
the floods will begin to recede.

Here it is: a clear sky.

Here it is: a rebuilding.

Here it is, at last: the sun.

MY GREAT-GRANDMOTHER DOES NOT REALLY KNOW MY AGE

but she always writes me a birthday card anyway,
always gets it in the ballpark at least.
The kind of love so vast it writes
to its second husband's great-granddaughter
every single year and means it.

Maybe she is the fortune teller
keeping me alive; she always thinks
I am older than I am,
like a promise:
here is tomorrow. I know
it will come.

Holding on is believing there's only a past;
letting go is knowing there's a future.

—DAPHNE ROSE KINGMA

NOTES

"Depression is Funny Like That" and "The Girl Becomes Gasoline" have both been featured on Button Poetry. Thank you for watching them.

"My Neighbor Votes for Donald Trump and I Cannot Help But Think of His Wedding Vows" is an erasure of traditional Christian wedding vows.

"*I need someone to save me | before I drive myself crazy | and if life is a dream | then so are we.*" —Mac Miller is a lyric from Mac Miller's song "I Can See" off his posthumous album *Circles*.

Mayor Duke won his fourth consecutive term in 2017, and passed away in 2019 at the age of 13, which is a year longer than the life expectancy of Great Pyrenees.

Mac Miller died on September 7th, 2018. Drew died on September 8th, 2018.

The poem "Mac Miller Dies Two Days Before You Do" is an erasure of the lyrics of Mac Miller's song, "Blue," also from his posthumous album.

ACKNOWLEDGEMENTS

THANK YOU to my parents, who always made sure I had books to read and a notebook to write in, and to my grandmother who taught me that writing is just as worthy as anything else. To my grandfather, who taught me quitting isn't an option. To Andrew and Katie, who taught me what kind of power my voice held. To Stacey, who didn't just believe in me, but pushed me to believe in myself. To Deborah, the high school English teacher who changed my life. To Sam, who has never stopped rooting for me from the moment we met. To Jo, for the comforting words and open arms when the writing got hard. To Livia, to Marissa, to Zainab, to DJ: this wouldn't be possible without you. To my LTAB team and to the Pause group piece, who made my passion a reality. To every friend who has showed up to my shows, even when they were small and they were the only ones in the audience. To you, for making all of this even possible. Thank you.

ABOUT THE AUTHOR

Reagan is the youngest Grand Slam champion to ever come out of Nebraska, and was the first woman to hold the title in seven years. She's been to two National Poetry Slams as a member of the Omaha team, founded and represented the University of Nebraska-Lincoln at the College Unions Poetry Slam Invitational for two years, and was the Woman of the World Poetry Slam Nebraska rep for 2016, in addition to being a member of different teams for regional competitions. You can see her work on Button Poetry, which has accumulated over 3.5 million views, and has also been written about in *The Huffington Post*, *Bustle*, and *Everyday Feminism*. She received her master's degree in composition and rhetoric from the University of Nebraska.

OTHER BOOKS BY BUTTON POETRY

If you enjoyed this book, please consider checking out some of our
others, below. Readers like you allow us to keep broadcasting
and publishing. Thank you!

Neil Hilborn, *Our Numbered Days*
Hanif Abdurraqib, *The Crown Ain't Worth Much*
Sabrina Benaim, *Depression & Other Magic Tricks*
Rudy Francisco, *Helium*
Rachel Wiley, *Nothing Is Okay*
Neil Hilborn, *The Future*
Phil Kaye, *Date & Time*
Andrea Gibson, *Lord of the Butterflies*
Blythe Baird, *If My Body Could Speak*
Desireé Dallagiacomo, *SINK*
Dave Harris, *Patricide*
Michael Lee, *The Only Worlds We Know*
Raych Jackson, *Even the Saints Audition*
Brenna Twohy, *Swallowtail*
Porsha Olayiwola, *i shimmer sometimes, too*
Jared Singer, *Forgive Yourself These Tiny Acts of Self-Destruction*
Adam Falkner, *The Willies*
Kerrin McCadden, *Keep This To Yourself*
George Abraham, *Birthright*
Omar Holmon, *We Were All Someone Else Yesterday*
Rachel Wiley, *Fat Girl Finishing School*
Nava EtShalom, *Fortunately*
Bianca Phipps, *crown noble*
Rudy Francisco, *I'll Fly Away*
Natasha T. Miller, *Butcher*
Kevin Kantor, *Please Come Off-Book*
Ollie Schminkey, *Dead Dad Jokes*

Available at buttonpoetry.com/shop and more!